Totally Silly
Jokes

by
Alison Grambs

Illustrated by
Rob Collinet

STERLING PUBLISHING CO., INC.
New York

*Dedicated to Acorn, Hef, the Cop,
and The New York Friars Club*

Published by Sterling Publishing Co., Inc.
387 Park Avenue South, New York, N.Y. 10016
© 2003 by Alison Grambs
Distributed in Canada by Sterling Publishing
C/o Canadian Manda Group, One Atlantic Avenue, Suite 105
Toronto, Ontario, Canada M6K 3E7
Distributed in Great Britain and Europe by Chris Lloyd at Orca Book Services,
Stanley House, Fleets Lane, Poole, BH1S 3AJ, England
Distributed in Australia by Capricorn Link (Australia) Pty. Ltd.
P.O. Box 704, Windsor, NSW 2756, Australia

Sterling ISBN 1-4027-0364-3

Contents

1. Old MacDonald Had a ...

What energy snack do chimps like?
Monkey bars.

Why are baby goats fun to play with?
They're always kidding around.

Why are fish easy to fool?
Because they're so gill-able.

Which sea creatures work out at the gym?
    Muscles.

What kind of sweaters do tortoises wear?
    Turtle-necks.

How can you tell a whale is sad?
    By its blubber-ing.

Why did the escargot visit the manicure salon?
    She needed to get her snails done.

What's a good name for an oyster?
Pearl.

What do fishermen do at a classical music concert?
Tuna piano.

What did the sea lion do before mailing his letter?
Seal the envelope.

How do bulls drive their cars?
With steer-ing wheels.

Where do pigs sleep in the summertime?
In ham-mocks.

What prehistoric animals eat in coffee shops?
Diner-saurs.

How did the crocodile get to the top of the building?
He took the ele-gator.

What's a good name for a Grizzly bear?
Teddy.

What's a good name for a duck?
Bill.

What bird wears a toupee?
A bald eagle.

Why is it so hard to move a parakeet?
Because they don't budge-y for anyone.

What bird lives in your throat?
A swallow.

Why didn't the duck like to go out to dinner?
It always got stuck with the bill.

How do felines carry their money?
In cat nap sacks.

What's a scientist's favorite dog?
The Lab.

What dog is the best swimmer?
A lap dog.

What did the dog do when he couldn't afford to buy a new car?
He leash-ed one.

What do you give a dog to make him laugh?
A funny bone.

What is a matador's favorite dog?
The bulldog.

Why didn't the dog get caught stealing the bone?
Because he flea-ed the scene before the cops showed up.

What do DVD players and dogs have in common?
They both have pause.

What animal makes the best butler?
A go-pher.

What insect is a good letter writer?
A spelling bee.

What police unit do flies fear most?
The SWAT team.

Where did the horse go for dinner?
To his nay-bor's house.

How do horses wear their hair in the summer?
In pony tails.

2. Where Would We Be Without...?

Why do spiders enjoy computers so much?
They like to play on the Web.

Why was the restaurant owner having a tough time getting his website running?
Because he didn't have a good server.

Why did the computer screen get in trouble with his mother?
Because he was a cursor.

How do flowers stay in touch on the Internet?
With their bud-dy lists.

Computers enjoy what popular snack?
Chip and dip.

How do you keep a computer's breath fresh?
Give it a docu-mint.

What music do computers like to dance to?
Disc-o.

Why did the computer call the exterminator?
It had a mouse.

What kind of shirt does a computer wear to school?
A lap-top.

Why did one font dump the other font?
He wasn't her type.

Why was the computer wearing a muzzle?
So it wouldn't byte.

Was the computer's road trip to California fun?
Yes, but it was a hard drive.

How does Raggedy Ann back up her computer files?
With a floppy disk.

What do you call it when you love your music
collection?
A CD Rom-ance.

How do computers get placed in honors classes?
They go through a screen-ing process.

Why did the VCR vacation at a fancy spa?
It needed to unwind.

What is the new way to cure a sick computer?
Treat it with modem medicine.

Where do DVD players like to vacation?
In remote islands.

Which television shows are the cleanest?
Soaps.

Which stereos give the finest lectures?
The ones with the best speakers!

Why did the old-fashioned camera find the digital camera so annoying?
Because she was always talking and he couldn't shutter up!

How do you borrow a camera?
Someone lens it to you.

Where did the camera take his date?
To a film.

Why aren't photographers fun to have around?
Because of their negative attitudes.

What do phone stores do?
They cell phones, duh!

What kind of machine gets in trouble for cussin'?
An answore-ing machine.

Why do answering machines run up such big bills at health spas?
Because they get lots of massages.

What do phones exchange when they get married?
  Rings.

How do prisoners stay in touch with each other?
  With their cell phones.

How do amoebas stay in touch with each other?
  With their cell phones.

Why didn't the other appliances like the fax?
  It was a bit phone-y.

How do you get off the phone with a closet?
You hang up.

What happened at the football game between the cell phones and the cordless phones?
The ref made a bad call.

Why do surgeons get so many phone calls?
Because they're big operators.

What do you send a telephone when it's one year old?
A birthday cord.

How do you get a book to come to the telephone?
  You page it.

Where do most telephones live?
  In Connect-icut.

What's the best way to get in touch with your mother?
  Beep-er.

What's a good name for an ATM machine?
  Rich.

Why do you need an ATM machine to make pizza?
That's where you get the dough, silly!

How do fingers communicate on a computer?
By e-nail.

How did the police officer stop the runaway refrigerator?
She yelled, "Freeze!"

3. Food for Thought

Why did the banana get a speeding ticket?
He got caught peeling out of the parking lot.

Why did the grapefruit get kicked out of the chorus?
He kept hitting sour notes.

How do you get two fruits to dance?
You pear them up.

What happens when a grape is getting old and cranky?
It starts to wine.

What fruit makes drinking easier?
The straw-berry.

What fruit unlocks doors?
The Ki-wi.

What's a good name for a fruit?
Barry.

Why did the police photograph the cup of coffee?
To get its mug shot.

What drink makes you go, "OUCH!"?
  Punch.

What types of jokes do farmers make?
  Corn-y ones.

LEM: Hey, did you hear about the new animated
    movie about the princess who falls in love with a
    vegetable farmer?
CLEM: Yup, it's called "Beauty and the Beets."

What did the carrot hope for on its vacation?
  Peas and quiet.

How do you send a bouquet to someone on
Mother's Day?
  You caul-i-flower shop.

What's the most adorable vegetable in the field?
  The cute-cumber.

What vegetable is kept in a cage?
  A zoo-chini.

Why was the lettuce a big success?
  He had a head for business.

How do you get a piece of bread to do you a favor?
  You butter it up.

What do you call a Southwestern dish that's been in the freezer?
A burrrr-ito.

How do loaves of bread congratulate each other?
With a toast.

What is a sailor's favorite sandwich?
A sub.

What is a soldier's favorite sandwich?
The hero.

Why does bread get fat?
Because it loafs around all day.

What noise do stolen hamburgers set off?
Burger alarms.

What's a clock's favorite meal?
Minute steak.

What kind of pasta has lots of pimples?
Zit-i.

What's a good snack to eat on Father's Day?
Pop-corn.

What egg wears cowboy boots?
A Western omelet.

Why couldn't the egg get good reception on his television?
All the channels were scrambled.

What's a good name for an egg?
Shelley.

What do you eat for lunch in a cemetery?
Tomb-atoes and grave-y.

Why don't detectives make good vegetarians?
Because they're always on steak-outs.

What's a good name for a hot dog?
  Frank.

What's a good name for a hamburger?
  Patty.

What language do cold cuts speak?
  Spam-ish.

Where does spaghetti go to dance?
  To a meat-ball.

Which sandwich tastes best at the beach?
  Peanut butter and jelly-fish.

On which day of the week does ice cream taste best?
  Sundae.

What dessert helps you drink your milk?
  Cup-cakes.

How does a piece of pie see the future?
  Through a crust-al ball.

What candy shrinks when you put it in the dryer?
  Cotton candy.

What happens if you put too many cocoa beans in
your mouth?
  You choke-a-lot.

What do sweet, old ladies walk with?
  Sugar canes.

What language do pastries speak?
  Danish.

What do balloons drink at birthday parties?
  Soda pop.

What candy do teeth love most?
  Gum-my bears.

What do poor squirrels hunt for in the winter?
  Dough-nuts.

What treat do they serve in prison?
Jail-y doughnuts.

Why didn't the doughnut like the brownie?
It was a bit nutty.

Why didn't the oatmeal cookie like the chocolate cookie?
It had a chip on its shoulder.

What is the sweetest Christmas song?
Frosting, the Snow Man.

When are newlyweds the sweetest ?
When they're on their honey-moon.

Why was everyone clapping for the bowl of rice?
Because it was puddin' on a great show.

4. Up, Up, Up and Away!

Why did the sun get straight A's?
Because it was very bright.

How did the chimney sweep get to California?
He flue on a plane.

How did the pilot fly without directions?
He just winged it.

Why did the helicopter turn around in mid-flight?
It felt propelled to do so.

What did the cow jump over?
The moooooo-n.

How do aliens get clean?
They take meteor showers.

What do you call aliens who do karate?
Martian arts experts.

What's the best way to see the constellations up close?
Climb up the star-case.

How do you keep an asteroid's hair looking nice?
You com-et.

Are the restaurants on Jupiter any good?
Well, the food is tasty, but the restaurants lack atmosphere.

How do you contact people on Saturn?
Give them a ring.

Where do NASA employees eat?
On the lunch pad.

What do NASA employees eat their lunches on?
Satellite dishes.

How does a hen have a baby hen?
She laser.

What space weapons are very chewy?
Laser gums.

How do you get a spaceship to sleep?
You rock-et.

How do you prepare for a trip to the Mars?
Plan-et well.

How did Mars take Venus to court?
It filed a space suit.

What mistake did the astronaut make?
He didn't consider the gravity of his situation.

Are astronauts as smart as they say?
For the most part, but they can be a bit space-y.

What's a good name for a molecule?
Adam.

5. Getting Around

What's a good name for a beach?
Sandy.

What's a good name for a church?
Abby.

What's a good name for a museum?
Art.

What's a good name for a place you exercise?
Jim.

What is the best thing to wear to a coffee bar?
A tea-shirt.

Why do reporters like to go to ice cream parlors?
Because that's where they get the scoops.

Why are bank tellers boring at parties?
They act very withdrawn.

What gender are many employees at the Post Office?
Mail.

Why are supermarkets a good place to meet dates?
You can always check out the possibilities.

Why are manicure salons so neat?
Because they have a good filing system.

How do you catch a street?
You corner it.

What do you call a London policeman?
Bobby.

What is the cleanest city in England?
Bath.

What do tired, sleepy New Yorkers knit with?
Yawn.

How do pieces of bread in Paris celebrate?
They make a French toast.

Where is the best place to celebrate Thanksgiving?
Turkey.

Where is the best place to buy fancy plates?
China.

What's the most popular holiday in Egypt?
Mummy's Day.

In what country do you always need a sweater?
Chile.

What flavor yogurt grows in the midwestern United States?
Plain.

Where do sharks go on vacation?
Finland.

What do Hawaiian cows wear to go out dancing?
Moo moos.

What people walk very fast?
Russians.

Where do giant sea creatures live?
In Wales.

What's a good name for a German motorcyclist?
Helmut.

What's a good name for a highway?
Miles.

What's the most important meal of the day for a car?
Brake-fast.

Why did the car pull over to the side of the road?
It was tire-d.

How does the Abominable Snowman commute?
On an ice-cycle.

Did the bicycle really win the debate?
Nope, it spoke too soon.

What scooter is always depressed?
A mope-ed.

What boat is always sorry for itself?
A woe-boat.

Why do passengers like shopping on board ship?
Because everything is on sail.

Are cars fascinating?
Yes, they're wheely, wheely interesting.

Is it expensive to take a taxi to the airport?
No, the rates are usually fare.

Why did the train get fired on its first day of work?
It got off on the wrong track.

6. Home Sweet Home

What's a nice gift to give a pastry chef?
Flours.

Where do flour and eggs meet?
At a mixer.

What happened when the pancake met the spatula?
She flipped for him.

How did critics rate the new cooking show on TV?
They pan-ned it.

Why did the stove quit its job?
It got burned out.

How did the cops get the barbecued chicken to confess?
They kept grilling her.

What utensils do construction workers eat with?
Fork lifts.

What do U.S. football linebackers eat cereal from?
A Super-bowl.

Why are refrigerators hard to make friends with?
Because they're very cool customers.

Where are refrigerators built?
In Chile.

Where did the dirt take his date?
To the dust-ball.

Why did the load of laundry quit its job?
Its career was all washed up.

What kind of bike does a washing machine ride?
A spin cycle.

How can you tell that a toilet bowl is embarrassed?
It gets all flushed.

What's a good name for a bathroom rug?
Matt.

Why was the toilet paper having such good luck?
It was on a roll.

Why is it so tiresome to fix a broken shower?
The work is very drain-ing.

Why was the stick of deodorant so depressed?
Its life was the pits.

KID: Dad, why are people so fussy about their shampoo?
DAD: Because it's hair today, gone tomorrow.

How do rabbits keep their hair in good shape?
With a hare conditioner.

What kind of mail do air conditioners receive?
Fan mail.

Why did the sponge quit his job?
His career was all dried up.

Why was the faucet so worried?
It had a sink-ing feeling.

What makes towels so funny?
They have a dry sense of humor.

How do mirrors pass the time?
Reflecting on the passing scene.

Are razors smart?
Yes, they're very sharp.

What was the curtain doing in the artist's studio?
It was being drawn.

Why was the picture frame late for the meeting?
It got hung up.

Why do water pitchers get facials?
To clean out their pours.

Why don't lamps get sunburned?
Because they're always in the shade.

How does a window get chosen for a house?
It has to be screened for the job.

Why don't doors like to play with windows?
Because windows are a pane in the neck.

What's a good name for a house plant?
Fern.

What's a good name for a nail?
Rusty.

What cases does a library judge try?
Book-cases.

What do the Library Police do?
They book people.

How do babies cheat on tests?
They use crib notes.

What should you sit on at a rock concert?
A rockin' chair.

How do ladders help your career?
They give you a step up.

What's a good name for a mattress?
Bette.

What did the pillow say to the crying comforter?
"Why are you so down?"

What furniture is seldom seen in public?
Your drawers.

What vegetable watches too much television?
  A couch potato.

What kind of chair wears a bracelet?
  An arm chair.

What is the oldest piece of furniture in the house?
  The grandfather clock.

What's a clock's favorite game?
  Tick-Tock-Toe.

What happened when the table played baseball?
It got bench-ed.

What furniture helps you do your math homework?
A count-er.

TOMMY: Hey Bill, how much voltage is in a light bulb?
BILL: Watt does it matter?

Why was the daughter mailbox mad at the daddy mailbox?
Because he wouldn't let-ter go to the mall.

JEFF: Hey, why did you throw out that calendar?
JENNIFER: Oh, it's a little out date-d.

Why did the broom stay up so late at night?
Because it had trouble falling a-sweep.

7. Bringin' Home the Bacon

What's a paramedic's favorite plant?
IV.

What is the key to becoming a successful doctor?
A lot of patients.

What kind of dentist works in the military?
A drill sergeant.

What's a good name for a mugger?
Rob.

What's a good name for a cook?
  Stu.

What's a good name for a lawyer?
  Sue.

How did the lobster become a lawyer?
  It went to claw school.

Why did the jury laugh at the lawyer?
  He was showing them his briefs.

What metal do robbers use to break into houses?
Steal.

What's a good name for a waiter?
Trey.

Why did the waitress call her stockbroker?
She was looking for a good tip.

Why did the waitress quit her job?
She didn't like taking orders.

What's a good name for a karaoke singer?
Mike.

What game do banks play?
Check-ers.

How do bank robbers get away from it all?
In a get-away car.

How did the janitor get fired?
He got caught sweeping on the job.

Why was the garbage man crying?
Because he got canned.

What makes an excellent baker?
One who caters to your every knead.

Who rescued the drowning pumpkin?
  The life-gourd.

How do sailors send packages to their families?
  They ship them.

What do politicians spread on their ham sandwiches?
  Mayor-naise.

How does a mailman stop a fire?
  He stamps it out.

8. Facing the Music

What instrument is most dangerous to play?
  The Bermuda Triangle.

Why was the piano locked out of its house?
  It lost its keys.

What musical instruments are donated to hospitals?
  Organs.

Why do musicians do so well in class?
  Because they take lots of notes.

What's a drummer's favorite part of a chicken?
  The drumstick.

Did the drum win the contest?
  No, it got beat.

What physical trait improves your violin playing?
  A clef chin.

How did the violin get into the orchestra?
  It pulled some strings.

Why was the big violin annoyed with the little violin?
  Because it was always fiddle-ing around.

Can you clean your teeth with a musical instrument?
Yes, use a tuba toothpaste.

What instrument boils hot water when you play it?
The kettle drum.

What vegetable plays the drums in a rock band?
The beet.

What seafood dish do saxophone players eat?
Blow-fish.

How did the trumpet do when he auditioned for the orchestra?
He blew it.

Why didn't Billy toss his kid sister in the air?
He didn't want to harm-Monica.

Why was the cello so upset?
It was only making a bass salary.

Which pants make beautiful music?
Bell bottoms.

What instrument do dogs play?
The trom-bone.

What instrument is ideal for shopping at the mall?
Bag-pipes.

What did the piccolo's mother tell her child?
"Don't piccolo your nose!"

9. Mother Nature

Why did the tree travel to his hometown?
He was searching for his roots.

Why did the tree's birthday party end so early?
The other trees started leaf-ing.

Why did the boy go to forestry camp?
He thought it wood be fun.

Why are movies about trees so silly?
The story lines are always sap-py.

What's the saddest tree of all?
The weeping willow.

Why did the tree sign up for extra classes?
It needed to branch out.

What did Noah use on the Ark to help him see at night?
Flood-lights.

What's a good name for a pond?
Lily.

Why did the flower enter the pageant?
She was a bud-ding beauty.

Is the soil on sale at the nursery?
Yep, and it's dirt cheap!

What candy do you find in swamps?
Marsh-mallows.

Where does water sleep?
In a river bed.

Where do they auction off bodies of water?
On E-bay.

What card game do you play over a river?
Bridge.

What weather do kings love?
Reign.

What weather do horses dislike?
Rein.

Did the farmer think there would be enough rain?
He had his droughts.

What happened when the knife and spoon took a hike ?
They came upon a fork in the road.

Where do pebbles go to listen to music?
To a rock concert.

Why is lightning so hard to catch?
Because it bolts.

What's a good name for a volcano?
Ash-ley.

When is the storm coming?
Monsoon-er or later.

What's a tornado's favorite game?
Twister.

Which natural disaster shows you lots of places around town?
A tour-nado.

What kind of storm is very spicy?
A Thai-phoon.

What kind of wave attacks bookstores?
A title wave.

What should you do in an ice storm?
Hail a cab.

Why won't someone tell you if an avalanche is coming?

What you don't snow won't hurt you.

What is Frosty the Snowman's favorite song?

"There snow business like show business…"

What do you hear when you drop an omelet in the Grand Canyon?

Egg-o, egg-o, egg-o.

10. We're Only Human

How does a cowboy catch a herd of runaway eyeballs?

He lash-oes them.

How do eyeballs fight?

They tend to lash out.

What should you wear on your legs at a baseball game?

Knee caps.

What kind of car does a rich knee drive?

A Bent-ly.

What happens if you park your foot in one place for too long?

It gets toe-d.

What fish smells like feet?

Filet of sole.

How come the foot was considered a miracle worker?

It had heel-ing powers.

What's a good name for a foot?

Arch-ie.

What's another good name for a foot?
Toe-ny.

What does a King's son always leave on the beach?
Foot-prince.

What part of the body makes a good pasta sauce?
The toe-mato.

What does the autobiography of a leg talk about?
Its thighs and lows.

What's the coolest part of the human body?
The hip.

Why did the fortune teller move to Florida?
She needed more palms to read.

What's a good way to carry barbecued food?
In a rib-cage.

MANAGER: How are sales for that new perfume?
SALESWOMAN: Scent-sational!

What's a good name for a guy with a furry chest?
Harry.

How does a chin cross the street?
First he looks to the right, then to the cleft.

What's a good name for a boy with a short haircut?
Bob.

What magazine do gardeners like to read?
Weeder's Digest.

What's a nose's favorite color?
Blew.

Why was the nose so poor?
It didn't have a scent to its name.

11. Keeping Score

How does a chef catch a baseball?
With an oven mitt.

Why is baseball the richest sport?
It's the only one played on a diamond.

How do you get water at a baseball game?
Ask for a pitcher.

Why was the insect such a bad baseball player?
It kept hitting fly-balls.

What sport makes a lot of noise at night?
Cricket.

What sports do nearsighted people play?
Contact sports.

Why was the tennis player told to quiet down?
He was making a racket.

What vegetable comes with a free racket?
Squash.

What kind of raft melts in water?
An ice cream float.

How do you decorate a rowboat for Christmas?
You hang oar-naments on it.

What type of shirt should oarsmen yachters wear?
Crew neck.

What boats talk too much?
Kay-yaks.

Why do people enjoy fishing so much?
It's a sport you can really get hooked on.

What did the scuba diver say when he was given more air?
"Tanks!"

Why are roller blades good to use?
Because they keep you in-line.

What's the best season for sky-diving?
Fall.

What sport do trains sign up for at school?
Track and field.

What sport is played on a carpet?
Rug-by.

What earrings do basketball players wear?
Hoops.

What sport is played in between two mountains?
Valley-ball.

What kind of parties do shoes attend?
Foot-balls.

Why did the football player buy a lawn mower?
He had a lot of yards to go.

What did the coach yell when the telephone didn't return his money?
"Hey! I want my quarter back!"

What snack do ducks serve at Superbowl parties?
Quackers and cheese.

Why didn't the hen go bungee cord jumping with the turkeys?
She was chicken.

Why are couches good to bungee jump with?
They cushion your fall.

How did the ski instructor get to the top of the mountain?
He got a lift.

What chairs are popular at tennis matches?
Love seats.

What do golfers wear at tournaments?
Tee shirts.

How do you learn to play golf?
Take a golf course.

What's a golfer's favorite lunch?
A club sandwich.

What happens when golfers gossip?
They can be very caddy.

Why did the polo player get in trouble?
He was horsing around on the field.

Why did the pool player take so long to make his shot?
He was waiting for his cue.

What's so great about running marathons?
They jog your memory.

12. Dressed to Chill

What's a good name for a denim jacket?
Jean.

What does a lawyer wear to court?
A law suit.

What do scientists wear to the lab?
Sneakers with test tube socks.

What do you call the marriage of two old socks?
Hole-y matrimony.

What kind of music do shoemakers love?
  Sole music.

How did the shoe salesman get his daughter into the movie without paying?
  He had to sneaker in.

Why did the cowboy leave his job at the shoe store?
  He got the boot.

What does a phone book wear to a fancy party?
  Ad-dress.

What do your clothes do when your closet is too full?

Oh, they just hang around.

What nutrient do clothes need?

Iron.

Why did the skirt end up in prison?

It pleated guilty.

Where do finger puppets get their outfits?

They're all hand-me-downs.

What do prizefighters wear under their clothes?

Boxer shorts.

How do you know a hat is in a good mood?

It's brim-ming with joy.

Why did the hat turn bad?

It was hanging out with a lot of hoods.

How did one mitten feel about the other mitten?

He was in glove with her.

Why were the pants dragged down to the police precinct?

They got cuffed.

What did the mother say to the book before it went outside to play?

"Don't forget to put on your jacket!"

What jackets do firefighters wear?

Blaze-ers.

How do you entertain a hemline?

Keep it in stitches.

What is a tie's favorite Shakespearean quote?

"To be or knot to be."

13. School Days

Why didn't the teacher call on the light bulb for answers?
Because it was a bit dim.

How can you get your ballpoint pen to march?
Yell, "Left! Write! Left, write, left!"

What's best to write with?
It de-pens.

What grade did the eyeball get in math this year?
C.

What class do snakes teach at school?
Hiss-tory.

What's your teacher's favorite dessert?
Chalk-o-late cake.

What is the best tool in the classroom?
The scissors ... they're a cut above the rest.

Where can toddlers plant flowers at school?
In the kinder-garden.

How do omelets get into school?
They have to pass an egg-zam.

Why are prisoners good at biology?
Because they know a lot about cells.

When are teachers most annoying?
When they get test-y.

When are teachers awesome?
When they have a lot of class.

Where in school are you most likely to catch a cold?
In the cough-ateria.

What cartoon character gets in trouble at school?
Suspended animation.

Where do you go to study art?
Collage.

What do future bankers love most in school?
Show 'n' Teller.

What do trees use to take notes at school?
Loose leafs.

What do baseball catchers get assigned a lot of?
Home work.

Why did the brush get grounded?
Because she didn't comb home by her curfew.

14. What's Up, Doc?

How did the cold spread?
It flu.

Where do you catch colds?
On a choo-choo train.

Why doesn't the chin like the nose?
The chin thinks the nose is stuffy.

Why did the ship sneeze?
It had a mast-y cold.

Why did the cow stay home with a cold?
  She was milking it for all it was worth.

Why did the Volkswagen go to the hospital?
  It had a bug.

Why did the computer stay home from school?
  It had a virus.

How can you tell your neck is angry?
  You've got a sore throat.

What kind of shots do sick hunters fire when they go hunting?
Flu shots.

What part of your body can finish a marathon?
Your runny nose.

How come the man is always burping?
He works at a gas station.

What allergy makes horses sneeze?
Hay fever.

How do you know when seafood makes you sick?
Your skin gets clammy.

BUNNY: Hey, doc, how bad is it?
DOCTOR: Well, you've got a hare-line fracture.

Why couldn't the foot afford to buy a new shoe?
Because it was broke.

How did the doctor tell her patient he broke his foot?
She braced him for the bad news.

What injury do bullfighters get?
Spain-ed ankles.

Why did the leaf go to the hospital?
It had a bad fall.

What do dogs fear most at the vet?
Getting a cat-scan.

Why did prehistoric people have such bad teeth?
Because they got a lot of cave-ities.

What disease do old roofs get?
Shingles.

What's a good name for an eye doctor?
Iris.

15. In Your Dreams

Why did the vampire see a therapist?
Because he was going batty.

Why did Dracula go to the doctor?
Because he couldn't stop coffin.

Where does Dracula brush his teeth?
In the bat-room like everyone else, silly!

How did the butcher kill the vampire?
He drove a steak through his heart.

What does Dracula wear on cold winter days?
His fang-ora sweater.

Which computer did Dracula buy?
The one with the most bytes.

Is Frankenstein a scary monster?
Yes! Of corpse, he is!

GHOST #1: Hey, why are you wearing that bandage on your finger?
GHOST #2: Oh, I got a boo boo.

What do goblins take to the beach on Halloween?
Sand-witches.

What is King Kong's favorite dessert?
Ape-le pie à la mode.

What do you call it when King Kong and Queen Kong have a fight?
Gorilla warfare.

Why did the King have to move to an uglier castle?
Because he got de-moat-ed.

What did Captain Hook say to Peter Pan after their fight?
"Ahoy, matey. Why don't you and eye patch things up and be friends?"

How do you get to a magical place?
Take a fairy boat ride.

How was the Easter Bunny's vacation?
Egg-cellent!

Will the Easter Bunny's injury heal?
Yes, the doctors are very hop-ful.

Why was the Easter Bunny late for the Easter Parade?
He was getting his hare done at the salon.

How was Captain Hook's surprise party?
Nice, but the crew went a little overboard with the decorations.

Why did Captain Hook get arrested?
He got caught pirating computer software.

What do pirates munch on while sailing the open seas?
Cans of sword-ines.

How does Santa tend to his crops?
With a ho, ho, ho.

How did the librarian tell Santa's helpers to be quiet?
"Sh-elves!"

What do elves surf on?
Micro-waves.

How do you measure a castle?
Use a ruler!

What did King Arthur say to Sir Lancelot as he was leaving the party?
"Good knight!"

Does Snow White have lots of friends?
Yeah, but one is a little Dopey.

Who makes a butterfly's wish come true?
  The Fairy Godmoth-er.

How does your dentist get to work each morning?
  He takes the Tooth Ferry.

What would Winnie the Pooh do after his wedding?
  Go on his honey-moon.

Why was the dragon depressed?
  He got fire-ed.

GENIE: Hey, doc, why do I feel so stressed out?
THERAPIST: Because your feelings are all bottled up!

What jewelry did the Headless Horseman get for his birthday?

A neck-less.

What animated film do eggs just adore?

"Poach-ahontas."

What type of sport utility vehicle would a dinosaur drive?

A Bronco-saurus.

BOY: What's your favorite part of the circus?
GIRL: The lion tamer act.
BOY: Why?
GIRL: Because it's the mane event.

16. Shore Thing

What does a waiter do at the beach?
He surfs food.

What does a beach ghost say?
"Buoy, oh buoy!"

What's a good name for the Sun?
Ray.

What do slow-talking people sit under at the beach?
An ummmmmmmbrella.

Why was the surfer dude yawning at the beach?
Because he was board.

What do clams do when it rains at the beach?
They seek shell-ter.

Why did the ocean's mother punish him?
Because he wasn't keeping his room tide-y.

What do fishing boats do when they catch the flu?
They make an appointment with the local dock.

What does a tropical fruit wear to the beach?
  A bikiwi.

What bikini got stuck in a chimney?
  The bathing soot.

What did the kneecap get when it went scuba diving?
  The bends.

What did the elephants wear to the beach?
  Trunks.

What do hamburgers do at the beach?
Build bun fires.

Where do movie stars vacation?
On a Tom Cruise ship.

How does seaweed move?
With a little kelp from its friends.

What does the ocean spread at Christmastime?
Good tide-ings.

Why was the ocean a lousy house guest?
Because it made a lot of long distance foam calls.

What does the ocean do to say goodbye?
Wave.

17. Try It Yourself!

Uh-oh! Looks like the end of the book! No more jokes to read. Hmmmmm. Better make up some of your own! It's as easy as pun, two, three! To get you started, you'll need a pencil and the idea for a punny joke, such as:

Why did the fisherman flunk his math test?
He wasn't _____ smart.

Now we need two punny words — two words that sound the same, but have different meanings — such as:

> word #1: real — something that is not fake
> word #2: reel — something attached to a fishing rod

Place both these words next to the Subject (the fisherman) and ask yourself this very important question, *"Which word do I think of when I think of a fisherman? 'Reel' or 'real'?"*

(Just in case you're not sure, the answer is "reel.")

Once you've made your decision, put word #1 (real) in the garbage and put the word #2 into the punch line. If you said:

"He wasn't reel smart."

you've just made up a punny joke!

Think you can do it? Give it a try! Come up with the word that will fit into the following punch lines on the next pages.

Good luck ... and have pun!

Subject: Does Tigger visit Winnie the Pooh often?

　　Word #1 hint — the type of animal Winnie the Pooh is.
　　Word #2 hint — another word meaning what you are when you're in the bathtub.

Now, pick the word that belongs with the Subject:

Punch line: Nope, they _____-ly see each other these days.

Word #2: bare

Subject: When does King Arthur eat dinner?

　　Word #1 hint — a medieval person who wears armor.
　　Word #2 hint — a time of day that is dark.

Now, pick the Word that belongs with the Subject.

Punch line: At _____.

Word #2: knight

Subject: How do you keep warm while painting in the winter?

Word #1 hint — what people wear in cold weather.
Word #2 hint — what painters call layers of paint.

Now, pick the word that belongs with the Subject.

Punch line: Wear extra _____.

Either word: coats

Subject: How do you get a boot to go away?

Word #1 hint — something you wear on your foot.
Word #2 hint — a kind of fly pie is made with it.

Now, pick the word that belongs with the Subject.

Punch line: You tell it to _____!

Word #1: shoe

About the Author

The daughter of two totally cool writers,
Alison Grambs works at The New York Friars Club.
Her acting credits include the National Tours of *Annie*
and *Chicago City Limits* as well as a bunch of
commercials no one ever saw. A graduate of
Haverford College, Alison lives in Manhattan with
her husband (a very strong policeman), their motor-
cycle, and two dogs who like to eat Chinese food.

About the Illustrator

Rob Collinet is an illustrator, filmmaker, and on-line
game designer. When doing none of the above he
can be found mountain biking, hiking, or sitting in
his backyard enjoying his garden. He, his wife (a
wedding cake designer), and their son live in Toronto,
Canada, with their Boston Terrier who dances for
treats and their cat who sleeps all day.

Index